Mental Health and Wellness Resource Booklet

Brampton

MACP Program, Yorkville University

PSYC: 6104: A Biopsychosocial Approach to Counselling

Samuel Gori

October, 2023

Authors' Profile

My name is Samuel Gori and my cultural background is South Asian. I was born and raised in Pakistan. I have been living Since Feb. 15, 2002, and I am privileged and honored to be a Canadian Citizen. I have had the great honor of working and teaching in the fields of Counselling, Theology, and Eschatology for more than 23 years. I have earned a year's degree in Civil Engineering from the Government College of Technology Lahore Pakistan. I have earned a four-year degree in Theology from Portland Bible College. I am a founder and Lead Pastor of All Nations Bible Church in Mississauga. I am also dean of students at Premillennial College in Mississauga, where I teach different subjects such as the foundation of Christian doctrines, Apocalyptic literature, hermeneutics, and so forth. Further, I am a theologian and author. I love history and I have the privilege and honor to write 21 books on the subject of Eschatology. It has been my dream and extreme desire to study Biopsychology. I must acknowledge that pursuing a Master of Arts in Counselling Psychology at Yorkville University was a dream that has come true.

Mental Health and Wellness Resource Booklet

Brampton

Samuel Gori

First Printing: 2023

ISBN: 9798864988411

Samuel Gori Publications

Ordering Information:
Special discounts are available on quantity purchases by corporations, associations, educators, and others. For details, contact the publisher at the above-listed address.

Dedicated to all the readers

And

City of Brampton.

Table of Contents

City of Brampton

A Brief History of Brampton, A flower City

The City of Brampton is known as the city of flowers and it is the third most expensive city in Canada. People have been living in this general area for centuries. Archaeological evidence confirms that native peoples had hunting camps and small villages along the Credit and Humber river valleys from about 8000 B.C.E.

European settlers began arriving in Ontario by the early 1780s. But, even into the early 1800s, Brampton was still wilderness, largely untouched by settlement. To prepare for the eventual influx, lands in Chinguacousy and Toronto Gore Townships were surveyed in 1818. Surveyors described the region as low, swampy, and covered with dense hardwood forest. Slowly land was cleared, cabins built and fields were ploughed for farming.

The historical heart of modern Brampton has always been the intersection of Queen and Main Streets, later known as the "four corners". This urban focal point has existed since the 1820s. Only a handful of people lived in the community at this time.

Another defining feature of the new settlement was Etobicoke Creek. The creek played its part in Brampton's development but because it was slow-moving and meandering, it could never sustain large-scale milling operations. The Brampton settlement grew more slowly as a result.

In the early 1820s, John Elliott settled in the village. He and another settler named William Lawson were staunch members of the Primitive Methodist movement and they established a strong Methodist presence in the area. Both were from Brampton, Cumberland, England. In 1834, they named the settlement Brampton in honor of their English home. Elliott also had village lots surveyed for sale to help attract other settlers. John Scott established the first industrial venture with an ashery used to produce potash.

By 1846 the village had two stores, a tavern, a tannery, a cabinetmaker, two blacksmiths, and two tailors, and the population had reached 150 people.

In 1853, Brampton was officially incorporated as a village. The population had grown to more than 500 people. Several churches were built, along with a grammar school, distilleries, several stores, and John Haggert's agricultural implements factory. The local economy was growing and the village supported the surrounding farms and rural hamlets.

The Grand Trunk Railway constructed a rail line and a station in Brampton in 1856. In the mid-Victorian era, the arrival of a railway line usually triggered an economic boom and Brampton was no different. By the 1860s the village was growing fast. In 1867,

Brampton was selected as the Peel County seat. The County Courthouse, Jail, and other public buildings were constructed. Kenneth Chisholm built Alderlea, a massive estate in the heart of the Village. Large homes were built near the Courthouse. Extensive land holdings surrounding the four corners were subdivided to build houses for the many new arrivals. Brampton was incorporated as a town in 1873 and John Haggert was elected the first Mayor.

A new industry was emerging in Brampton by the mid-Victorian era. In 1860, Edward Dale established a flower nursery. Within a few short years, Brampton became known as the "Flower Town of Canada" and soon Dale's Nursery was Brampton's largest employer. By the turn of the century, hundreds of acres of land were filled with greenhouses growing prize orchids, hybrid roses, and many other quality flowers. Most of these flowers were grown for export around the world.

The 20th century brought new industries to the town, mostly along the railway line, including the Williams Shoe factory, the Copeland-Chatterson Loose-Leaf Binder company, and the Hewetson Shoe factory. Major banks established branches on the four corners. In 1907, American industrialist Andrew Carnegie established a library in the downtown and the population reached 4,000 people by 1910.

Brampton's citizens endured two world wars and the Great Depression during the first half of the 20th century. These major world events took their toll on the local economy. Some factories closed and the flower industry began a slow but steady decline.

The City slowly transformed after the Second World War. In the late 1940s and 1950s, the automobile began to change the landscape, as did rapid urban growth in Toronto. New subdivisions began to develop. In the late 1950s, Bramalea was created and touted as "Canada's first satellite city". Bramalea was a planned community built to accommodate 50,000 people by integrating houses, shopping centers, parks, commercial businesses, and industry.

In March 1948, Brampton endured a devastating flood when Etobicoke Creek overflowed its banks. The creek flooded repeatedly, but the 1948 flood was considered the worst. The town launched an ambitious civil engineering project to straighten and reroute the creek. Construction of a concrete diversion channel began in June 1950. Premier Leslie Frost officially opened it on July 5, 1952.

In 1974, the Region of Peel was created and Brampton became a city. Large-scale and leading-edge industries located in Brampton. In the 1980s and 1990s, large subdivisions developed on lands formerly used for farming. The culturally diverse and vibrant City of today was emerging.

Brampton is now among the largest urban centers in Canada with a population of over 603,346 People (2017) United Nations. The roots of Brampton's success can be traced to its heritage. The foundations were first laid almost 200 years ago when a group of industrious people established a small hamlet at the crossroads of Queen and Main Streets.

Source: https://www.brampton.ca/EN/Arts-Culture-Tourism/Tourism-Brampton/

Introduction

Defining Biopsychosocial

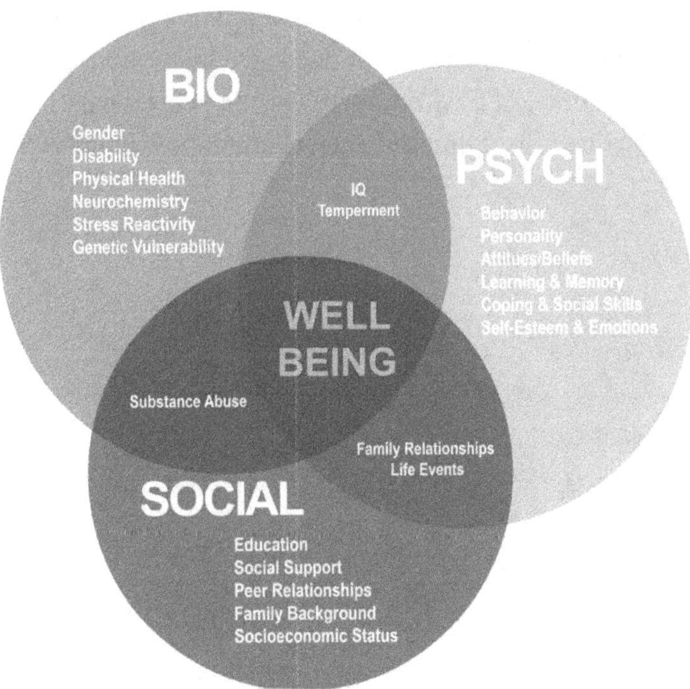

A biopsychosocial framework for counseling psychology that draws upon the physical, mental, and social health disciplines creates an interdisciplinary model from these three pillars. This model is illustrated through the examination of selected counseling issues, such as anxiety, depression, attention deficit hyperactivity disorder, and neurocognitive factors.

Source: https://courses.yorkvilleu.ca/course

Biopsychology is the scientific study of the biology of behavior (Dewsbury 1991) Biopsychology is a unique combination of biopsychological science and personal read-oriented discourse. (John P. J. Pinel & Steven J. Barnes, 2021)

Biopsychosocial Approach to Mental health and wellness

Biopsychosocial refers to the use of biological, psychological, and social principles to address human wellness and health. The Biopsychosocial (BPS) Model suggests that significant interaction among the three disciplines affects why and how distress or illness occurs.

Source:

https://study.com/academy/lesson/what-is-the-biopsychosocial

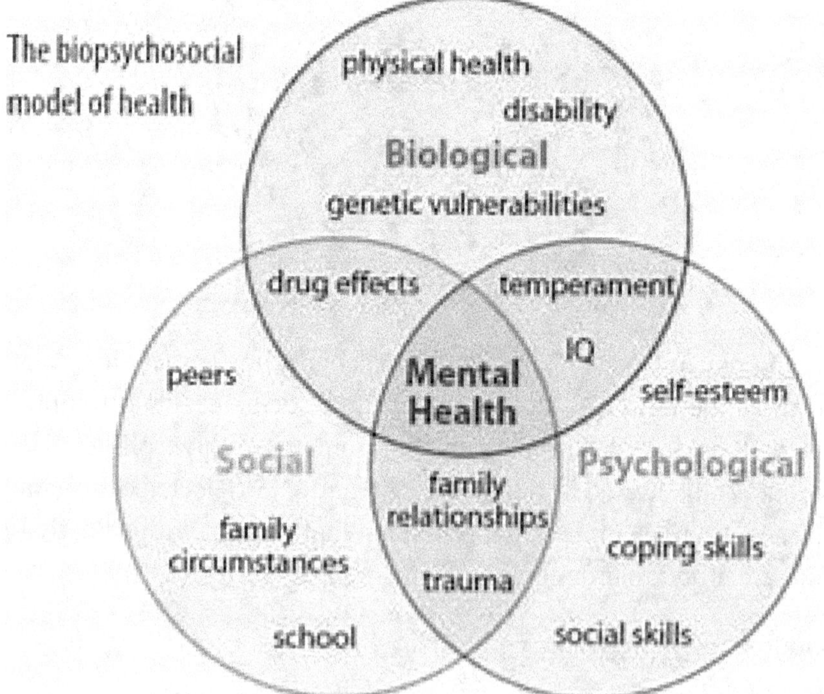

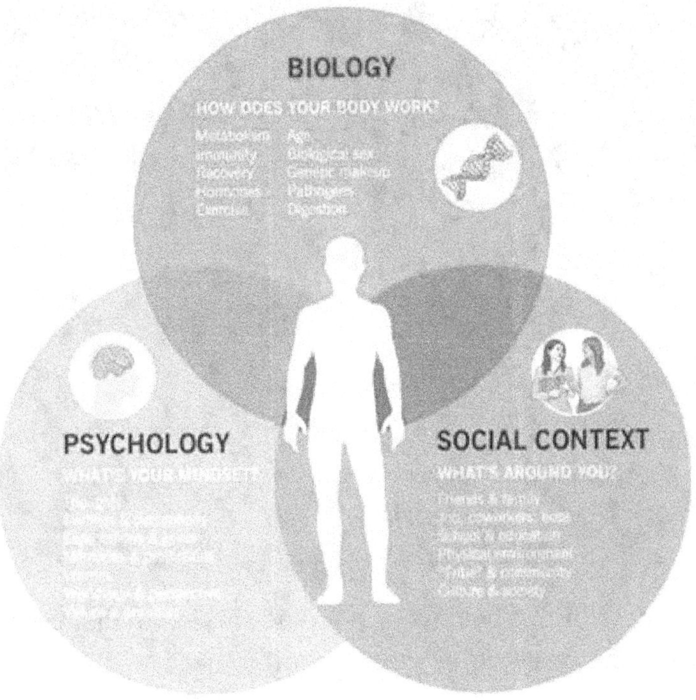

Source: https://www.bing.com/images/search?q=Biopsychosocia

Purpose of this Booklet?

The purpose of this booklet is to provide access to the resources in the City of Brampton. Counselors often need to refer clients to community services, programs, agencies, specialists, etc. that provide specialized support and guidance for individuals and families. The information provides a brief overview of the resources, services, and fees, and if medical referrals are required to activate the services listed. Mental health services also reduce the risk of chronic diseases related to stress, anxiety, and substance abuse. Most importantly, mental health services save lives, while improving the outlook for people who may feel hopeless and lost. This booklet will help me look for a potential Practicum placement site near the end of my MACP program.

Resources – Brampton

1. Intervention for Depression

FVB Psychologists

The psychologists, psychological associates, and therapists at FVB Psychologists are trained to assess and treat a wide range of psychological problems including:

- anxiety-based disorders, e.g., generalized anxiety, social anxiety, obsessive-compulsive disorder, panic, and posttraumatic stress disorder (e.g., the psychological response to motor vehicle accidents, assault, or sexual abuse).
- mood disorders such as major depressive disorder and dysthymic disorder.
- interpersonal conflicts including marital or relationship problems and family conflict.
- the loss of a loved one through death, separation, or divorce.
- chronic pain management.
- sexual dysfunction.
- vocational and/or rehabilitation challenges.
- anger management.
- assertiveness training.
- stress management.
- LGBTQ+ challenges.
- adjustment disorders.

Treatment Services

- ➢ Grief and Loss
- ➢ Couples Therapy

> ➢ Chronic Pain / Rehabilitation
> ➢ Intervention for Anxiety
> ➢ Intervention for Depression
> ➢ Trauma
> ➢ Child and Family Services

Assessment Services

> ➢ Psychoeducational Assessments
> ➢ Psychology

First Responders - police

Contact

Brampton Office

7685 Hurontario Street, Suite 505<

Brampton, ON L6W 0B4

Brampton: (905) 793-8858

Fax: (905) 793-8134

Email: infob@fvb.ca

https://www.fvb.ca/services/

·········
·········

The Family Enhancement Centre
Counselling Services Brampton

Mental health service in Brampton, Ontario

Located in: Springdale Village Centre

Address: 2250 Bovaird Dr E #603, Brampton, ON L6R 0W3

Hours:

Closed · Opens 9 a.m.

Phone: (905) 799-2228

Appointments: tfec.ca

Province: Ontario

2. Trauma and PTSD, Addiction and Anxiety

Tharshiga Elankeeran

Registered Psychotherapist, MA, RP (she, her)

Verified by Psychology Today 3 Endorsed

It is my honor to sit in the passenger's seat while you control the steering wheel of your life. Despite all the chaos you may have been through, I firmly believe that you are the expert on you. With all that happens, sometimes we lose ourselves and live a life incongruent with our values. Naturally, we start to feel depressed, anxious, angry, etc. I assist and empower your true essence for you to make life-affirming decisions that align with your values, and ultimately live a wholehearted life. We surpass focusing on the issue that brought you into therapy, to making and reaching life goals.

My Practice at a Glance

Brampton, ON L6Y

(647) 370-0282

https://www.psychologytoday.com/ca/therapists/tharshiga-elankeeran-brampton

At this time of massive changes, so much is unknown. How will you choose to respond? I am available for video sessions only at this time.

I specialize in Trauma and PTSD, Addiction, and Anxiety

I see individuals, couples, and groups

3. Mental Health and Wellness Services

NATASHA COUNSELLING

Natasha Ramzan Social Work Professional Corporation

Services

- Online Therapy
- Individual Therapy

---

1 hr Fee for Services

Couples/Family Therapy

---

1 hr 30 min

Student Therapy

---

1 hr

Group Therapy

Dialectical Behaviour Therapy Skills Group

---

90 minutes

Cognitive Behavioural Therapy Group

Email: admin@natashacounselling.com

https://www.natashacounselling.com/services-1

4. Suicide Prevention, Addiction, and Mental Health

Hope by CAMH

10 Gillingham Dr #305,
Brampton, ON L6X 5A5

Brampton Office:
905-792-0821

Crisis Line:
1-800-810-0180

info@hope247.ca

:::::::::::::::::::::::::::
:::::::::::::::::::::::::::

Peel Region Plus

If you are in crisis and need help right now, please contact Peel Children's Centre's Crisis Line at 416-410-8615 (if under 18), 24.7 Crisis Line Peel at 905-278-9036 (if over 18), Kids Help Phone at 1-800-668-6868, or call 911.   The Region of Peel is home to approximately 1.5 million people. The cities of Brampton and the town of Caledon make up the Peel Region. Peel Region is also part of the Greater Toronto Area (GTA), which includes Toronto, and neighboring regions of Durham, Halton/Halton Hills, and York. We have included some resources from the GTA as well as Mississauga as these are areas of interest that we may want to live in and work in the future.

here is a central point of intake for Children and Youth called "Where To Start" Also, listed is the Canadian Mental Health Association (CMHA) which offers mental health services for all.

Following these resources are varied and specialized areas of support listed alphabetically in the Peel Region and GTA section.

Canadian Mental Health Association

Mental Health for All

Address: 7700 Hurontario St #314, Brampton, ON L6Y 4M3

Phone: (905) 451-2123

Province: Ontario

https://cmhapeeldufferin.ca/get-involved/careers/

Canadian Mental Health Association
At the Canadian Mental Health Association – Peel Dufferin Branch, we provide support and services to those who suffer from mental illness. As part of our team, you'll be empowered to make a bigger impact than you ever imagined – from assisting people who are struggling to help them return to good health. That's why we've made it a priority to create a diverse organization that represents the communities we serve. We're proud to do this important work – and we're especially honored to have received the Canadian Non-Profit Employer of Choice Award for our efforts in making the world a better place.

We Drive Equitable Recruitment Processes
Here at CMHA we are committed to diverse, inclusive, barrier-free recruitment, selection processes, and work environment. We encourage applications from members of groups that have been historically disadvantaged and marginalized. We acknowledge that removing existing barriers and preventing new barriers is required in providing opportunities that foster independence, inclusion, and dignity for people of all ages, genders, cultures,

and abilities. As an equal-opportunity employer, we are committed to establishing a qualified workforce that is reflective of the diverse population we serve.

CMHA Programs and Services

Our Unique Perspective
For over 55 years, the Canadian Mental Health Association – Peel Dufferin Branch (CMHA Peel Dufferin) has been a pioneer in providing services for people with mental illness and educating Canadians about mental health issues. As the leading client-driven, community-based mental health organization serving the Region of Peel and Dufferin County, we are innovative partners in proactively strengthening individual support, and developing a responsive mental health system.

CMHA Peel Dufferin champions good mental health for everyone and supports the full participation of those with mental illness and addictions in the life of the community. In addition to providing a variety of mental health and addiction services, we are committed to community development, mental health awareness, and addressing the stigma and discrimination surrounding mental illness.

Crisis Support Peel Dufferin
Get Help and Stay Safe in a Crisis If you are in a mental health crisis, we can help. Open 24 hours a day, 7 days a week. Call us…

Access to Recovery

Central Intake: 905-451-2123 Access to Recovery supports individuals experiencing long-term mental health concerns to lead fulfilling, satisfying lives within their community. What is Access to Recovery? Access to Recovery…

Assertive Community Treatment Team (ACTT)

The Assertive Community Treatment Team (ACTT) is a client-centered; recover-oriented mental health service that offers a broad range of intensive community support to individuals experiencing serious mental health…

Behavioral Supports Ontario Program

What is the Behavioral Supports Ontario Program? The Behavioural Supports Ontario (BSO) initiative was created to enhance health care services for older adults in Ontario with complex and responsive behaviors.

Brief Services – Family Support

CMHA Peel Dufferin offers support to those who are concerned about someone's mental health and substance use issues. Who could benefit? Family members struggling to understand and cope with the…

Brief Services – Mental Health Counselling

CMHA Peel Dufferin offers free Brief Mental Health Counselling services. Our program follows a brief counseling model that offers an immediate opportunity for therapeutic conversation within 1-2 sessions.

Brief Services – Substance Use

CMHA Peel Dufferin offers a Brief Services Substance Use Program at no cost to those who are seeking assistance with cutting down or stopping substance use and "addictive" behaviors. Who…

Case Management – Dufferin

What is Case Management? The goal of Dufferin Case Management is to promote support independence and improve quality of life, helping the person on a path to recovery.…

Concurrent Disorders Support Group

Concurrent Disorder Support Group is a support group for clients struggling with Addiction and Mental Illness. It is an open, peer support group with a psychoeducational component. Some…

Counseling and Treatment – Dufferin

The Mental Health Counsellors provide 6-8 sessions (once every 3-4 weeks). Goals for counseling are guided by the OCAN and are recovery-oriented. Who can benefit? Adults over the age…

Davidson Scholarship Fund

The Davidson Scholarship Fund provides financial support to individuals experiencing mental health concerns to pursue education. What is the Davidson Scholarship Fund? The Davidson Scholarship Fund was established through a bequest…

Dialectical Behavioral Therapy

Dialectical Behavioral Therapy (DBT) is an evidence-based structured psychotherapy. It is different than traditional talk therapies that are more process-oriented because the emphasis is on behavior changes to help improve a…

Early Intervention

Early Intervention supports individuals who have experienced a first episode of psychosis to lead fulfilling, satisfying lives within their community. What is Early Intervention? Early Intervention is provided in a...

Education and Training
Canadian Mental Health Association Peel Dufferin offers workshops open to the general public and organizations. We also offer workshops in the community, and onsite at your location. Our training...

Groups
CMHA Peel Dufferin offers mental health and addiction group programs for adults in our service area. You do not need to be a member of our programs to attend,...

Impact
Impact provides youth with substance abuse education and harm reduction strategies in individual and group settings. Support is also offered to connect youth to community resources. What is Impact? Impact...

In-STED
The In-STED program aims to identify complex mental health and addiction needs early and intervene through timely, high-quality, integrated, and culturally appropriate short-term case management services. What is the In-STED...

McEvenue Home Works
You can help individuals with mental illness and their families make it through a housing crisis by donating to this vital program. Just click here and include "McEvenue Home Works" in...

Mental Health and Justice

CMHA Peel Dufferin offers a range of mental health supports to individuals experiencing mental health concerns, who conflict with the law. Court Support Referral Form Release From Custody…

Outreach

What is the Peel Outreach Program? Peel Outreach Services offers a continuum of Housing Support that seeks to end homelessness in the Peel Region and increase access to mainstream services.…

Rapid Access Addiction Medicine Clinic (RAAM Clinic)

The Rapid Access Addiction Medicine Clinic (RAAM Clinic) provides low-barrier immediate access and care for substance use management. The clinic is accessible without appointments or medical referrals. The RAAM Clinic…

Recovery West

What is Recovery West? At Recovery West we believe that everyone in recovery from mental health issues should have support from their peers and a variety of opportunities throughout their…

Seniors at Risk System Coordination – Dufferin

Designed to assist in providing a safe short-term solution for clients who are being neglected or abused until a longer-term plan can be developed and implemented with a…

Seniors Intensive Case Management – Dufferin

This program is for Seniors who are experiencing serious and persistent mental health concerns. Seniors having challenges accessing support due to geography, isolation, or changes in informal support system are…

Specialized Geriatric Service – Dufferin

An assessment and treatment program for Dufferin seniors who are experiencing age-related cognitive decline due to dementia, depression, delirium, or pharmacological reasons. Who can benefit? Anyone experiencing age-related cognitive...

Supported Housing

Supported Housing offers permanent housing, and supports individuals experiencing mental health concerns to lead fulfilling, satisfying lives within their community. What is Supported Housing? Supported Housing offers intensive community-based supportive...

SystemWise

Where everyone comes together to support one person's needs. Within the various sectors of Social Services exist mechanisms for System Coordination. While each sector may refer to the process by...

Transitional Aged Youth (TAY) Program Treat at Home

Treat at Home supports older adults experiencing mental health concerns to lead fulfilling, satisfying lives within their community. What is Treat at Home? Treat at Home offers intensive community-based...

Vocational Support Services

Vocational Support Services offers assistance with recovery goals around employment, education, and volunteer opportunities through individual and group support. For information on our Davidson Scholarship Fund

314-7700 Hurontario Street

Brampton ON L6Y 4M3

Phone: (905) 451-2123

E-mail: info@cmhapeel.ca

Facebook: https://www.facebook.com/CMHAPeel

Flickr Flickr: https://www.flickr.com/photos/123706804@N06/

Twitter Twitter: https://twitter.com/CMHAPeelRegion

Website Website: cmhapeeldufferin.ca

YouTube YouTube: https://www.youtube.com/channel/UCxfXc36m9A9vZpSV1IvTVhA